50 Perfect Seasonal Cooking Recipes

By: Kelly Johnson

Table of Contents

- Roasted Butternut Squash Soup
- Pumpkin Spice Bread
- Apple Cinnamon Pancakes
- Grilled Corn on the Cob
- Roasted Root Vegetables
- Strawberry Rhubarb Pie
- Summer Caprese Salad
- Grilled Peach Salad
- Watermelon Feta Salad
- Sweet Potato Casserole
- Apple Crisp
- Zucchini Fritters
- Lemon Basil Pasta
- Spaghetti Squash with Pesto
- Tomato Basil Soup
- Peach Cobbler
- Grilled Shrimp Tacos
- Baked Salmon with Lemon and Dill
- Braised Beef Short Ribs

- Carrot Cake
- Roasted Beet Salad with Goat Cheese
- Grilled Vegetable Skewers
- Blackberry Crumble
- Pumpkin Risotto
- Cornbread Stuffing
- Creamy Garlic Mashed Potatoes
- Sweet Corn Soup
- Fresh Mango Salsa
- Grilled Chicken Caesar Salad
- Baked Apple and Pear Crumble
- Chilled Cucumber Soup
- Roasted Chicken with Herb Butter
- Pecan Pie
- Cranberry Sauce
- Cabbage and Kielbasa Skillet
- Spicy Pumpkin Soup
- Fresh Tomato Bruschetta
- Shrimp and Grits
- Roasted Garlic and Herb Potatoes
- Spinach and Artichoke Dip

- Baked Stuffed Bell Peppers
- Lemon Meringue Pie
- Baked Frittata with Seasonal Veggies
- Grilled Pineapple with Honey
- Eggplant Parmesan
- Apple and Walnut Salad
- Maple Glazed Carrots
- Grilled Lamb Chops
- Sweet Potato Fries
- Roasted Brussel Sprouts with Bacon

Roasted Butternut Squash Soup

Ingredients:

- 1 medium butternut squash, peeled and cubed
- 1 onion, chopped
- 2 garlic cloves, minced
- 2 tbsp olive oil
- 4 cups vegetable broth
- 1/2 cup coconut milk
- 1 tsp ground ginger
- 1/2 tsp ground cinnamon
- Salt and pepper to taste
- Fresh thyme for garnish (optional)

Instructions:

1. Preheat the oven to 400°F (200°C).
2. Toss the cubed butternut squash, chopped onion, and garlic in olive oil, and season with salt and pepper.
3. Spread the mixture on a baking sheet and roast for 25-30 minutes until the squash is tender and caramelized.
4. Transfer the roasted vegetables to a pot and add vegetable broth, coconut milk, ginger, and cinnamon.
5. Bring to a simmer over medium heat, then blend the soup with an immersion blender or in batches using a regular blender.
6. Adjust seasoning to taste and serve with fresh thyme.

Pumpkin Spice Bread

Ingredients:

- 1 3/4 cups (220g) all-purpose flour
- 1 tsp baking soda
- 1/2 tsp ground cinnamon
- 1/2 tsp ground nutmeg
- 1/2 tsp ground ginger
- 1/4 tsp ground cloves
- 1/2 tsp salt
- 1/2 cup (120ml) vegetable oil
- 1 cup (200g) sugar
- 2 eggs
- 1 cup (240g) pumpkin puree
- 1 tsp vanilla extract
- 1/2 cup (120ml) milk

Instructions:

1. Preheat the oven to 350°F (175°C) and grease a loaf pan.
2. In a bowl, whisk together flour, baking soda, spices, and salt.
3. In a separate bowl, beat together oil, sugar, eggs, and pumpkin puree.
4. Stir in the dry ingredients, followed by the vanilla and milk.
5. Pour the batter into the prepared loaf pan and bake for 55-60 minutes until a toothpick comes out clean.

6. Let cool before slicing and serving.

Apple Cinnamon Pancakes

Ingredients:

- 1 1/2 cups (190g) all-purpose flour
- 2 tbsp sugar
- 1 tsp baking powder
- 1/2 tsp baking soda
- 1 tsp ground cinnamon
- 1/4 tsp salt
- 3/4 cup (180ml) buttermilk
- 1/2 cup (120ml) milk
- 1 egg
- 1 tsp vanilla extract
- 1 apple, peeled and diced
- Butter or oil for cooking

Instructions:

1. In a bowl, combine flour, sugar, baking powder, baking soda, cinnamon, and salt.
2. In another bowl, whisk together buttermilk, milk, egg, and vanilla.
3. Pour the wet ingredients into the dry ingredients and stir until just combined.
4. Gently fold in the diced apple.
5. Heat a skillet over medium heat and lightly grease with butter or oil.
6. Pour 1/4 cup of batter onto the skillet for each pancake, cooking for 2-3 minutes per side until golden.

7. Serve with syrup and additional apple slices if desired.

Grilled Corn on the Cob

Ingredients:

- 4 ears of corn, husked
- 2 tbsp olive oil
- Salt and pepper to taste
- Lime wedges (optional)

Instructions:

1. Preheat the grill to medium-high heat.
2. Brush the corn with olive oil and season with salt and pepper.
3. Grill the corn for 10-15 minutes, turning occasionally until charred and tender.
4. Serve with lime wedges if desired.

Roasted Root Vegetables

Ingredients:

- 2 carrots, peeled and cut into chunks
- 2 parsnips, peeled and cut into chunks
- 1 sweet potato, peeled and cubed
- 1 red onion, cut into wedges
- 2 tbsp olive oil
- 1 tsp dried thyme
- Salt and pepper to taste

Instructions:

1. Preheat the oven to 400°F (200°C).
2. Toss all vegetables with olive oil, thyme, salt, and pepper.
3. Spread the vegetables on a baking sheet in a single layer.
4. Roast for 25-30 minutes, flipping halfway through, until golden and tender.

Strawberry Rhubarb Pie

Ingredients:

- 2 cups strawberries, hulled and sliced
- 2 cups rhubarb, chopped
- 1 1/2 cups sugar
- 1/4 cup cornstarch
- 1 tbsp lemon juice
- 1 tsp vanilla extract
- 1 package pie crusts (store-bought or homemade)

Instructions:

1. Preheat the oven to 375°F (190°C).
2. In a bowl, combine strawberries, rhubarb, sugar, cornstarch, lemon juice, and vanilla.
3. Roll out one pie crust and fit it into a pie dish.
4. Pour the fruit mixture into the crust and cover with the second crust.
5. Trim and crimp the edges, and cut small slits in the top crust.
6. Bake for 45-50 minutes until the crust is golden and the filling is bubbling.
7. Let cool before serving.

Summer Caprese Salad

Ingredients:

- 2 cups cherry tomatoes, halved
- 1 cup fresh mozzarella, torn into pieces
- 1/4 cup fresh basil leaves, torn
- 2 tbsp balsamic vinegar
- 1 tbsp olive oil
- Salt and pepper to taste

Instructions:

1. In a large bowl, combine tomatoes, mozzarella, and basil.
2. Drizzle with balsamic vinegar and olive oil.
3. Season with salt and pepper, and toss gently to combine.
4. Serve chilled.

Grilled Peach Salad

Ingredients:

- 4 peaches, halved and pitted
- 2 cups mixed greens
- 1/4 cup feta cheese, crumbled
- 1/4 cup walnuts, toasted
- 2 tbsp balsamic glaze

Instructions:

1. Preheat the grill to medium heat.
2. Grill the peach halves for 3-4 minutes per side until charred and softened.
3. Arrange the greens on a platter and top with grilled peaches, feta, and walnuts.
4. Drizzle with balsamic glaze and serve.

Watermelon Feta Salad

Ingredients:

- 4 cups watermelon, cubed
- 1/2 cup feta cheese, crumbled
- 1/4 cup fresh mint leaves, chopped
- 1 tbsp olive oil
- 1 tbsp lime juice
- Salt and pepper to taste

Instructions:

1. In a large bowl, combine watermelon, feta, and mint.
2. Drizzle with olive oil and lime juice, and season with salt and pepper.
3. Toss gently and serve chilled.

Sweet Potato Casserole

Ingredients:

- 4 large sweet potatoes, peeled and cubed
- 1/2 cup (120ml) milk
- 1/4 cup (60g) butter, melted
- 1/2 cup (100g) brown sugar
- 1 tsp vanilla extract
- 1/2 tsp cinnamon
- 1/4 tsp nutmeg
- 1/2 cup (60g) mini marshmallows (optional)

Instructions:

1. Preheat the oven to 375°F (190°C).
2. Boil the sweet potatoes in water until tender, about 15-20 minutes. Drain.
3. Mash the sweet potatoes with milk, melted butter, brown sugar, vanilla, cinnamon, and nutmeg.
4. Transfer to a greased baking dish and top with marshmallows, if desired.
5. Bake for 20-25 minutes until the top is golden and bubbly.

Apple Crisp

Ingredients:

- 4 cups apples, peeled, cored, and sliced
- 1 tbsp lemon juice
- 1/2 cup (100g) sugar
- 1 tsp ground cinnamon
- 1/2 cup (60g) rolled oats
- 1/2 cup (60g) all-purpose flour
- 1/4 cup (50g) brown sugar
- 1/4 cup (60g) butter, cubed

Instructions:

1. Preheat the oven to 350°F (175°C).
2. Toss the sliced apples with lemon juice, sugar, and cinnamon, then place them in a greased baking dish.
3. In a separate bowl, combine oats, flour, brown sugar, and butter. Use a pastry cutter or fork to mix until crumbly.
4. Sprinkle the oat mixture evenly over the apples.
5. Bake for 40-45 minutes until the top is golden and the apples are tender.

Zucchini Fritters

Ingredients:

- 2 medium zucchinis, grated
- 1/2 cup (60g) all-purpose flour
- 1/4 cup (25g) grated Parmesan cheese
- 1 egg, beaten
- 1/4 tsp garlic powder
- Salt and pepper to taste
- Olive oil for frying

Instructions:

1. Grate the zucchini and squeeze out excess moisture with a towel.
2. In a bowl, combine the zucchini, flour, Parmesan, egg, garlic powder, salt, and pepper.
3. Heat olive oil in a pan over medium heat.
4. Drop spoonfuls of the zucchini mixture into the pan and flatten slightly.
5. Fry for 3-4 minutes per side until golden brown.
6. Drain on paper towels and serve.

Lemon Basil Pasta

Ingredients:

- 8 oz pasta (spaghetti or linguine)
- 1 tbsp olive oil
- 2 cloves garlic, minced
- 1/2 cup fresh basil, chopped
- Zest and juice of 1 lemon
- Salt and pepper to taste
- Grated Parmesan cheese for serving

Instructions:

1. Cook pasta according to package instructions. Drain and reserve 1/4 cup of pasta water.
2. In a large pan, heat olive oil over medium heat and sauté garlic for 1-2 minutes.
3. Add the cooked pasta, basil, lemon zest, and juice to the pan. Toss to combine.
4. Add reserved pasta water to achieve desired consistency.
5. Season with salt and pepper, and serve with grated Parmesan.

Spaghetti Squash with Pesto

Ingredients:

- 1 medium spaghetti squash
- 1/2 cup pesto (store-bought or homemade)
- Salt and pepper to taste
- Fresh basil leaves for garnish

Instructions:

1. Preheat the oven to 375°F (190°C).
2. Cut the spaghetti squash in half and remove the seeds.
3. Place the squash halves cut-side down on a baking sheet and roast for 40-45 minutes until tender.
4. Using a fork, scrape the squash to create spaghetti-like strands.
5. Toss the squash with pesto and season with salt and pepper.
6. Garnish with fresh basil and serve.

Tomato Basil Soup

Ingredients:

- 6 cups canned crushed tomatoes
- 1 onion, chopped
- 2 cloves garlic, minced
- 2 tbsp olive oil
- 2 cups vegetable broth
- 1 tsp dried basil
- Salt and pepper to taste
- Fresh basil leaves for garnish
- 1/4 cup heavy cream (optional)

Instructions:

1. In a large pot, heat olive oil over medium heat and sauté the onion and garlic until softened, about 5 minutes.
2. Add crushed tomatoes, vegetable broth, dried basil, salt, and pepper.
3. Bring to a simmer and cook for 20-25 minutes.
4. Use an immersion blender or regular blender to puree the soup until smooth.
5. Stir in heavy cream if using, and garnish with fresh basil.

Peach Cobbler

Ingredients:

- 4 cups fresh or frozen peaches, sliced
- 1/2 cup (100g) sugar
- 1 tsp lemon juice
- 1 cup (125g) all-purpose flour
- 1/2 cup (100g) sugar
- 1 1/2 tsp baking powder
- 1/4 tsp salt
- 1/2 cup (120ml) milk
- 1/4 cup (60g) butter, melted

Instructions:

1. Preheat the oven to 375°F (190°C).
2. In a bowl, toss the peaches with sugar and lemon juice, then spread them in a greased baking dish.
3. In a separate bowl, combine flour, sugar, baking powder, salt, milk, and melted butter.
4. Pour the batter over the peaches, spreading evenly.
5. Bake for 40-45 minutes until the top is golden and the peaches are bubbling.

Grilled Shrimp Tacos

Ingredients:

- 1 lb (450g) shrimp, peeled and deveined
- 2 tbsp olive oil
- 1 tsp chili powder
- 1 tsp garlic powder
- 1/2 tsp cumin
- Salt and pepper to taste
- Small tortillas
- Toppings: avocado, cilantro, lime, sour cream, or salsa

Instructions:

1. Preheat the grill to medium-high heat.
2. Toss the shrimp in olive oil, chili powder, garlic powder, cumin, salt, and pepper.
3. Grill the shrimp for 2-3 minutes per side until pink and opaque.
4. Serve the shrimp in tortillas with desired toppings.

Baked Salmon with Lemon and Dill

Ingredients:

- 4 salmon fillets
- 1 lemon, sliced
- 2 tbsp fresh dill, chopped
- 2 tbsp olive oil
- Salt and pepper to taste

Instructions:

1. Preheat the oven to 400°F (200°C).
2. Place the salmon fillets on a baking sheet and drizzle with olive oil.
3. Season with salt and pepper, and top with lemon slices and dill.
4. Bake for 12-15 minutes until the salmon is cooked through and flakes easily with a fork.

Braised Beef Short Ribs

Ingredients:

- 4-6 beef short ribs
- 2 tbsp olive oil
- 1 onion, chopped
- 2 carrots, chopped
- 2 celery stalks, chopped
- 4 garlic cloves, minced
- 2 cups beef broth
- 1 cup red wine
- 2 tbsp tomato paste
- 1 bay leaf
- 2 tsp thyme
- Salt and pepper to taste

Instructions:

1. Preheat the oven to 325°F (165°C).
2. Heat olive oil in a large Dutch oven over medium-high heat. Season the short ribs with salt and pepper, and sear them on all sides until browned. Remove the ribs and set aside.
3. Add onion, carrots, celery, and garlic to the pot and sauté for 5 minutes until softened.
4. Stir in tomato paste and cook for 2 minutes.
5. Pour in the wine and beef broth, scraping up any browned bits from the bottom of the pot. Add the bay leaf and thyme.

6. Return the ribs to the pot, cover, and transfer to the oven. Braise for 2.5-3 hours until the ribs are tender and fall off the bone.

7. Serve with mashed potatoes or roasted vegetables.

Carrot Cake

Ingredients:

- 2 cups (240g) all-purpose flour
- 1 1/2 tsp baking powder
- 1/2 tsp baking soda
- 1/2 tsp salt
- 2 tsp ground cinnamon
- 1/2 tsp ground nutmeg
- 4 large eggs
- 1 1/2 cups (300g) sugar
- 1 cup (240ml) vegetable oil
- 2 tsp vanilla extract
- 3 cups (300g) grated carrots
- 1/2 cup (60g) walnuts or pecans, chopped (optional)

Cream Cheese Frosting:

- 8 oz (225g) cream cheese, softened
- 1/2 cup (115g) butter, softened
- 4 cups (450g) powdered sugar
- 1 tsp vanilla extract

Instructions:

1. Preheat the oven to 350°F (175°C). Grease and flour two 9-inch round cake pans.

2. In a bowl, combine flour, baking powder, baking soda, salt, cinnamon, and nutmeg.

3. In a separate large bowl, whisk eggs, sugar, oil, and vanilla until well combined.

4. Stir in the dry ingredients, then fold in grated carrots and nuts.

5. Pour the batter into the prepared pans and bake for 30-35 minutes until a toothpick comes out clean.

6. For the frosting, beat together cream cheese and butter until smooth, then gradually add powdered sugar and vanilla.

7. Cool the cakes completely before frosting. Frost the cakes and serve.

Roasted Beet Salad with Goat Cheese

Ingredients:

- 4 medium beets, peeled and cubed
- 2 tbsp olive oil
- Salt and pepper to taste
- 4 cups mixed greens
- 1/2 cup goat cheese, crumbled
- 1/4 cup walnuts, toasted
- 2 tbsp balsamic vinaigrette

Instructions:

1. Preheat the oven to 400°F (200°C).
2. Toss the beet cubes with olive oil, salt, and pepper, and spread them on a baking sheet. Roast for 25-30 minutes until tender, stirring halfway through.
3. In a large bowl, combine mixed greens, roasted beets, goat cheese, and toasted walnuts.
4. Drizzle with balsamic vinaigrette and toss to combine. Serve immediately.

Grilled Vegetable Skewers

Ingredients:

- 1 zucchini, sliced
- 1 bell pepper, chopped
- 1 red onion, chopped
- 8 oz (225g) mushrooms, whole or halved
- 1 pint cherry tomatoes
- 2 tbsp olive oil
- 1 tbsp balsamic vinegar
- 1 tsp garlic powder
- Salt and pepper to taste

Instructions:

1. Preheat the grill to medium-high heat.
2. Thread the vegetables onto skewers, alternating them.
3. In a small bowl, whisk together olive oil, balsamic vinegar, garlic powder, salt, and pepper.
4. Brush the vegetable skewers with the marinade.
5. Grill for 8-10 minutes, turning occasionally, until the vegetables are tender and slightly charred.
6. Serve as a side dish or with rice.

Blackberry Crumble

Ingredients:

- 4 cups fresh blackberries
- 1/2 cup (100g) sugar
- 1 tbsp lemon juice
- 1/2 cup (60g) all-purpose flour
- 1/2 cup (50g) rolled oats
- 1/4 cup (50g) brown sugar
- 1/4 tsp cinnamon
- 1/4 tsp salt
- 1/4 cup (60g) butter, cubed

Instructions:

1. Preheat the oven to 375°F (190°C).
2. Toss blackberries with sugar and lemon juice, then place them in a greased baking dish.
3. In a separate bowl, combine flour, oats, brown sugar, cinnamon, and salt.
4. Cut in butter until the mixture is crumbly.
5. Sprinkle the crumble topping over the blackberries.
6. Bake for 30-35 minutes until the topping is golden brown and the berries are bubbling. Serve warm with ice cream.

Pumpkin Risotto

Ingredients:

- 1 cup Arborio rice
- 2 tbsp olive oil
- 1 small onion, chopped
- 2 cloves garlic, minced
- 2 cups (480ml) vegetable broth
- 1/2 cup (120ml) white wine
- 1 cup (240g) pumpkin puree
- 1/4 cup (60ml) heavy cream
- 1/2 cup (50g) Parmesan cheese, grated
- Salt and pepper to taste
- Fresh sage leaves for garnish (optional)

Instructions:

1. Heat olive oil in a large pan over medium heat. Add the onion and garlic, cooking until softened, about 5 minutes.
2. Add the Arborio rice and cook for 1-2 minutes, stirring occasionally.
3. Pour in the white wine and cook until absorbed.
4. Gradually add the vegetable broth, 1/2 cup at a time, stirring constantly until the liquid is absorbed before adding more.
5. Once the rice is tender and creamy, stir in the pumpkin puree and heavy cream.
6. Remove from heat and stir in Parmesan cheese. Season with salt and pepper.

7. Garnish with fresh sage leaves, if desired.

Cornbread Stuffing

Ingredients:

- 1 batch cornbread, crumbled (about 6 cups)
- 1 tbsp olive oil
- 1 onion, chopped
- 2 celery stalks, chopped
- 2 cloves garlic, minced
- 1/2 cup (120ml) chicken broth
- 1 tsp dried thyme
- Salt and pepper to taste
- 1/4 cup fresh parsley, chopped

Instructions:

1. Preheat the oven to 350°F (175°C).
2. In a large pan, heat olive oil over medium heat. Sauté the onion, celery, and garlic for 5-7 minutes until softened.
3. In a large bowl, combine the crumbled cornbread with the sautéed vegetables, chicken broth, thyme, salt, and pepper.
4. Transfer to a greased baking dish and cover with foil. Bake for 20-25 minutes, then remove the foil and bake for an additional 10 minutes to crisp the top.
5. Garnish with fresh parsley and serve.

Creamy Garlic Mashed Potatoes

Ingredients:

- 4 large potatoes, peeled and cubed
- 3 cloves garlic, minced
- 1/2 cup (120ml) heavy cream
- 1/4 cup (60g) butter
- Salt and pepper to taste

Instructions:

1. Boil potatoes in salted water for 15-20 minutes until tender. Drain and return to the pot.
2. In a small saucepan, heat heavy cream and butter until melted and warm.
3. Mash the potatoes with a potato masher or hand mixer, adding the garlic, cream, butter, salt, and pepper.
4. Serve warm.

Sweet Corn Soup

Ingredients:

- 4 cups fresh or frozen corn kernels
- 1 onion, chopped
- 2 cloves garlic, minced
- 2 tbsp olive oil
- 4 cups vegetable broth
- 1 cup (240ml) milk
- 1 tsp thyme
- Salt and pepper to taste

Instructions:

1. Heat olive oil in a large pot over medium heat. Sauté onion and garlic for 5 minutes until softened.
2. Add corn, vegetable broth, milk, and thyme. Bring to a simmer and cook for 15 minutes.
3. Use an immersion blender to blend the soup until smooth, or blend in batches.
4. Season with salt and pepper, and serve hot.

Fresh Mango Salsa

Ingredients:

- 2 ripe mangoes, peeled and diced
- 1/2 red onion, finely chopped
- 1 red bell pepper, diced
- 1 jalapeño, finely chopped (optional for heat)
- 1/4 cup fresh cilantro, chopped
- Juice of 1 lime
- Salt and pepper to taste

Instructions:

1. In a bowl, combine diced mango, onion, bell pepper, and jalapeño.
2. Add the chopped cilantro, lime juice, salt, and pepper, and mix well.
3. Serve immediately with chips, tacos, or grilled meats.

Grilled Chicken Caesar Salad

Ingredients:

- 2 chicken breasts
- 1 tbsp olive oil
- Salt and pepper to taste
- 4 cups romaine lettuce, chopped
- 1/2 cup Caesar dressing
- 1/4 cup grated Parmesan cheese
- Croutons (optional)

Instructions:

1. Preheat the grill to medium-high heat. Rub chicken breasts with olive oil, salt, and pepper.
2. Grill the chicken for 5-7 minutes on each side until fully cooked. Let rest before slicing.
3. In a large bowl, toss the lettuce with Caesar dressing and Parmesan cheese.
4. Add sliced chicken on top and garnish with croutons if desired. Serve immediately.

Baked Apple and Pear Crumble

Ingredients:

- 2 apples, peeled and sliced
- 2 pears, peeled and sliced
- 1/4 cup brown sugar
- 1 tsp cinnamon
- 1/2 tsp nutmeg
- 1 tbsp lemon juice
- 1/2 cup rolled oats
- 1/4 cup all-purpose flour
- 1/4 cup butter, cubed
- 1/4 cup brown sugar (for topping)

Instructions:

1. Preheat the oven to 350°F (175°C).
2. In a bowl, toss the apples and pears with brown sugar, cinnamon, nutmeg, and lemon juice.
3. Transfer the fruit mixture to a greased baking dish.
4. In another bowl, mix oats, flour, butter, and brown sugar until crumbly. Sprinkle over the fruit.
5. Bake for 40-45 minutes until the top is golden and the fruit is bubbling.
6. Serve warm with ice cream or whipped cream.

Chilled Cucumber Soup

Ingredients:

- 2 cucumbers, peeled and chopped
- 1 cup Greek yogurt
- 1/2 cup sour cream
- 1/4 cup fresh dill, chopped
- 2 tbsp lemon juice
- 1 garlic clove, minced
- Salt and pepper to taste

Instructions:

1. In a blender, combine cucumbers, Greek yogurt, sour cream, dill, lemon juice, and garlic.
2. Blend until smooth. Add salt and pepper to taste.
3. Chill for at least 2 hours before serving. Garnish with extra dill and a squeeze of lemon.

Roasted Chicken with Herb Butter

Ingredients:

- 1 whole chicken (about 4 lbs)
- 1/4 cup butter, softened
- 2 tbsp olive oil
- 2 cloves garlic, minced
- 1 tbsp fresh thyme, chopped
- 1 tbsp fresh rosemary, chopped
- Salt and pepper to taste
- 1 lemon, halved

Instructions:

1. Preheat the oven to 400°F (200°C).
2. In a small bowl, mix butter, olive oil, garlic, thyme, rosemary, salt, and pepper.
3. Rub the herb butter mixture all over the chicken.
4. Place the lemon halves inside the cavity of the chicken.
5. Roast the chicken for 1.5 hours, or until the internal temperature reaches 165°F (75°C).
6. Let rest for 10 minutes before carving.

Pecan Pie

Ingredients:

- 1 1/2 cups pecans
- 1 cup light corn syrup
- 1 cup brown sugar
- 1/4 cup butter, melted
- 3 large eggs
- 1 tsp vanilla extract
- 1/4 tsp salt
- 1 pie crust, unbaked

Instructions:

1. Preheat the oven to 350°F (175°C).
2. In a large bowl, whisk together corn syrup, brown sugar, melted butter, eggs, vanilla, and salt.
3. Stir in the pecans.
4. Pour the filling into the unbaked pie crust.
5. Bake for 45-50 minutes until the pie is set and golden.
6. Cool before slicing.

Cranberry Sauce

Ingredients:

- 12 oz fresh cranberries
- 1 cup sugar
- 1 cup water
- 1/2 tsp orange zest (optional)

Instructions:

1. In a saucepan, combine cranberries, sugar, and water.
2. Bring to a boil, then simmer for 10-15 minutes until the cranberries burst and the sauce thickens.
3. Stir in orange zest if using, and remove from heat.
4. Let cool before serving.

Cabbage and Kielbasa Skillet

Ingredients:

- 1/2 head of cabbage, shredded
- 1 lb kielbasa, sliced
- 1 onion, chopped
- 2 tbsp olive oil
- 1/2 tsp caraway seeds (optional)
- Salt and pepper to taste

Instructions:

1. In a large skillet, heat olive oil over medium heat. Add onion and kielbasa, and cook until the kielbasa is browned.
2. Add the cabbage and caraway seeds (if using). Cook, stirring occasionally, until the cabbage wilts and becomes tender, about 10-15 minutes.
3. Season with salt and pepper, and serve warm.

Spicy Pumpkin Soup

Ingredients:

- 2 cups pumpkin puree
- 1 medium onion, chopped
- 2 cloves garlic, minced
- 1 tbsp olive oil
- 4 cups vegetable broth
- 1 tsp ground ginger
- 1/2 tsp ground cinnamon
- 1/4 tsp cayenne pepper
- Salt and pepper to taste

Instructions:

1. Heat olive oil in a large pot over medium heat. Add onion and garlic, and sauté until softened, about 5 minutes.
2. Add the pumpkin puree, vegetable broth, ginger, cinnamon, cayenne pepper, salt, and pepper.
3. Bring to a simmer and cook for 15 minutes, stirring occasionally.
4. Blend the soup with an immersion blender or in batches until smooth.
5. Serve hot, garnished with a dollop of sour cream if desired.

Fresh Tomato Bruschetta

Ingredients:

- 4 ripe tomatoes, chopped
- 1/2 cup fresh basil, chopped
- 1/4 cup balsamic vinegar
- 2 tbsp olive oil
- 1 baguette, sliced
- Salt and pepper to taste

Instructions:

1. Preheat the oven to 375°F (190°C). Arrange the baguette slices on a baking sheet and toast in the oven for 5-7 minutes until golden.
2. In a bowl, combine tomatoes, basil, balsamic vinegar, olive oil, salt, and pepper.
3. Spoon the tomato mixture onto the toasted baguette slices.
4. Serve immediately as an appetizer.

Shrimp and Grits

Ingredients:

- 1 lb shrimp, peeled and deveined
- 1 tbsp olive oil
- 1 garlic clove, minced
- 1/2 tsp smoked paprika
- 1/2 tsp cayenne pepper (optional)
- 1 cup grits
- 4 cups chicken broth
- 1/2 cup heavy cream
- 1/2 cup cheddar cheese, shredded
- Salt and pepper to taste
- 2 tbsp fresh parsley, chopped

Instructions:

1. Cook the grits according to the package instructions, using chicken broth for extra flavor. Once cooked, stir in the heavy cream, cheddar cheese, salt, and pepper. Keep warm.

2. In a large skillet, heat olive oil over medium heat. Add garlic and cook for 1 minute until fragrant.

3. Add shrimp to the skillet and cook for 3-4 minutes until pink. Season with paprika, cayenne pepper (if using), salt, and pepper.

4. Serve the shrimp over the grits, garnished with fresh parsley.

Roasted Garlic and Herb Potatoes

Ingredients:

- 1 lb baby potatoes, halved
- 3 tbsp olive oil
- 4 garlic cloves, minced
- 1 tbsp fresh rosemary, chopped
- 1 tbsp fresh thyme, chopped
- Salt and pepper to taste

Instructions:

1. Preheat the oven to 400°F (200°C).
2. In a large bowl, toss the halved potatoes with olive oil, garlic, rosemary, thyme, salt, and pepper.
3. Spread the potatoes on a baking sheet in a single layer.
4. Roast for 25-30 minutes, or until the potatoes are golden and tender, flipping halfway through.
5. Serve warm as a side dish.

Spinach and Artichoke Dip

Ingredients:

- 1 10 oz package frozen spinach, thawed and drained
- 1 can (14 oz) artichoke hearts, drained and chopped
- 1 cup cream cheese, softened
- 1/2 cup sour cream
- 1/2 cup mayonnaise
- 1 cup mozzarella cheese, shredded
- 1/2 cup Parmesan cheese, grated
- 2 garlic cloves, minced
- Salt and pepper to taste

Instructions:

1. Preheat the oven to 375°F (190°C).
2. In a large bowl, mix together spinach, artichokes, cream cheese, sour cream, mayonnaise, mozzarella, Parmesan, garlic, salt, and pepper.
3. Transfer the mixture to a baking dish and spread it evenly.
4. Bake for 20-25 minutes, until bubbly and golden on top.
5. Serve with chips, crackers, or sliced baguette.

Baked Stuffed Bell Peppers

Ingredients:

- 4 large bell peppers, tops cut off and seeds removed
- 1 lb ground beef or turkey
- 1 cup cooked rice
- 1/2 cup onion, chopped
- 1 can (14.5 oz) diced tomatoes
- 1 tsp garlic powder
- 1 tsp cumin
- 1 tsp chili powder
- 1/2 cup shredded cheddar cheese
- Salt and pepper to taste

Instructions:

1. Preheat the oven to 375°F (190°C).
2. In a skillet, cook the ground meat with onions over medium heat until browned, about 7-10 minutes.
3. Stir in cooked rice, diced tomatoes, garlic powder, cumin, chili powder, salt, and pepper. Cook for another 5 minutes.
4. Stuff the bell peppers with the mixture and place them in a baking dish.
5. Cover with foil and bake for 25-30 minutes.
6. Remove foil, top with cheese, and bake for an additional 5-10 minutes until the cheese is melted.

Lemon Meringue Pie

Ingredients:

- 1 pie crust, baked
- 1 1/2 cups granulated sugar
- 1/4 cup cornstarch
- 1/4 tsp salt
- 1 1/2 cups water
- 4 large egg yolks, beaten
- 1/2 cup fresh lemon juice
- 2 tbsp lemon zest
- 1 tbsp butter
- 4 large egg whites
- 1/4 tsp cream of tartar
- 6 tbsp granulated sugar

Instructions:

1. Preheat the oven to 350°F (175°C).

2. In a saucepan, combine sugar, cornstarch, and salt. Gradually add water and cook over medium heat, stirring constantly, until thickened.

3. Gradually whisk some of the hot mixture into the beaten egg yolks, then return everything to the pan. Cook for another 2-3 minutes, stirring continuously.

4. Remove from heat and stir in lemon juice, lemon zest, and butter. Pour the lemon filling into the baked pie crust.

5. In a separate bowl, beat the egg whites and cream of tartar until soft peaks form. Gradually add sugar and beat until stiff peaks form.

6. Spread the meringue over the lemon filling and bake for 10-12 minutes until golden. Let cool before serving.

Baked Frittata with Seasonal Veggies

Ingredients:

- 8 large eggs
- 1/2 cup milk
- 1 cup seasonal veggies (such as zucchini, bell peppers, spinach, or mushrooms)
- 1/2 cup cheese (cheddar, feta, or mozzarella)
- 1 tbsp olive oil
- Salt and pepper to taste

Instructions:

1. Preheat the oven to 375°F (190°C).
2. In a large oven-safe skillet, heat olive oil over medium heat. Add the veggies and cook until tender, about 5-7 minutes.
3. In a bowl, whisk together eggs, milk, salt, and pepper. Pour the mixture over the cooked vegetables in the skillet.
4. Sprinkle cheese over the top.
5. Bake for 15-20 minutes until the eggs are set and lightly golden on top.
6. Serve warm, cut into wedges.

Grilled Pineapple with Honey

Ingredients:

- 1 pineapple, peeled and sliced into rings
- 2 tbsp honey
- 1/4 tsp ground cinnamon (optional)

Instructions:

1. Preheat the grill to medium-high heat.
2. Brush the pineapple rings with honey and sprinkle with cinnamon if desired.
3. Grill the pineapple for 2-3 minutes on each side until grill marks appear and the pineapple is tender.
4. Serve immediately as a sweet side or dessert.

Eggplant Parmesan

Ingredients:

- 2 medium eggplants, sliced into 1/2-inch rounds
- 1 1/2 cups breadcrumbs
- 1/2 cup grated Parmesan cheese
- 2 cups marinara sauce
- 2 cups mozzarella cheese, shredded
- 1/4 cup fresh basil, chopped
- 2 eggs, beaten
- 1/2 cup all-purpose flour
- Olive oil for frying
- Salt and pepper to taste

Instructions:

1. Preheat the oven to 375°F (190°C).
2. In a shallow bowl, combine breadcrumbs, Parmesan cheese, salt, and pepper. In another bowl, place flour, and in a third, beat the eggs.
3. Dip each eggplant slice first in the flour, then the egg, and finally the breadcrumb mixture.
4. Heat olive oil in a large skillet over medium heat. Fry the eggplant slices for about 2 minutes on each side, until golden. Drain on paper towels.
5. In a baking dish, spread a thin layer of marinara sauce. Place a layer of fried eggplant slices, followed by more marinara sauce and mozzarella cheese. Repeat layers.
6. Top with fresh basil. Bake for 25 minutes or until the cheese is bubbly and golden.

Apple and Walnut Salad

Ingredients:

- 4 cups mixed greens (arugula, spinach, or lettuce)
- 1 apple, sliced
- 1/2 cup toasted walnuts
- 1/4 cup crumbled blue cheese (optional)
- 2 tbsp balsamic vinaigrette
- 1 tbsp olive oil
- Salt and pepper to taste

Instructions:

1. In a large bowl, toss mixed greens with sliced apple and toasted walnuts.
2. Drizzle with balsamic vinaigrette and olive oil.
3. Top with crumbled blue cheese (if using), salt, and pepper. Toss gently and serve immediately.

Maple Glazed Carrots

Ingredients:

- 1 lb baby carrots, peeled
- 2 tbsp maple syrup
- 1 tbsp butter
- 1 tsp fresh thyme, chopped
- Salt and pepper to taste

Instructions:

1. In a large pot, bring water to a boil and cook the carrots for 10-12 minutes, until tender. Drain.
2. In a skillet, melt butter over medium heat. Add the carrots, maple syrup, thyme, salt, and pepper.
3. Stir well to coat the carrots in the glaze and cook for 5-7 minutes, allowing the glaze to thicken.
4. Serve warm as a side dish.

Grilled Lamb Chops

Ingredients:

- 8 lamb chops
- 2 tbsp olive oil
- 2 garlic cloves, minced
- 1 tbsp fresh rosemary, chopped
- 1 tbsp fresh thyme, chopped
- Salt and pepper to taste

Instructions:

1. Preheat the grill to medium-high heat.
2. In a small bowl, mix olive oil, garlic, rosemary, thyme, salt, and pepper. Rub the mixture onto both sides of the lamb chops.
3. Grill the lamb chops for 4-5 minutes per side for medium-rare or to your desired level of doneness.
4. Let rest for 5 minutes before serving.

Sweet Potato Fries

Ingredients:

- 2 large sweet potatoes, peeled and cut into fries
- 2 tbsp olive oil
- 1/2 tsp paprika
- 1/2 tsp garlic powder
- Salt and pepper to taste

Instructions:

1. Preheat the oven to 425°F (220°C).
2. Toss the sweet potato fries in olive oil, paprika, garlic powder, salt, and pepper.
3. Spread the fries in a single layer on a baking sheet.
4. Bake for 20-25 minutes, flipping halfway through, until crispy and golden. Serve hot.

Roasted Brussel Sprouts with Bacon

Ingredients:

- 1 lb Brussels sprouts, trimmed and halved
- 4 slices bacon, chopped
- 2 tbsp olive oil
- Salt and pepper to taste

Instructions:

1. Preheat the oven to 400°F (200°C).
2. In a large skillet, cook the chopped bacon over medium heat until crispy. Remove from the skillet and set aside, reserving the bacon fat.
3. Toss the Brussels sprouts in olive oil, bacon fat, salt, and pepper. Spread them in a single layer on a baking sheet.
4. Roast for 20-25 minutes, flipping halfway through, until crispy on the edges.
5. Top with the crispy bacon and serve warm.

www.ingramcontent.com/pod-product-compliance
Lightning Source LLC
LaVergne TN
LVHW081320060526
838201LV00055B/2379